How to be a
Good
Lover

W0115418

Bodleian Library
UNIVERSITY OF OXFORD

This edition first published in 2012 by the Bodleian Library
Broad Street
Oxford OX1 3BG

www.bodleianbookshop.co.uk

ISBN: 978 1 85124 280 1

This edition © Bodleian Library, University of Oxford, 2012
Originally published as *Dos and Don'ts for Lovers*, by Universal
Publications, in 1936.
Images adapted from illustrations in Army and Navy catalogues
from 1930, 1933 and 1934 taken from the John Johnson
Collection in the Bodleian Library, University of Oxford;
Women's Clothes and Millinery 8 (23), (24) and (25) respectively.

Cover design by Dot Little
Designed and typeset in Georgia (9.5pt on 11.7pt) by
JCS Publishing Services Ltd, www.jcs-publishing.co.uk.
Printed and bound in China by C&C Offset Printing Co. Ltd on
100gsm YuLong pure 1.3

British Library Catalogue in Publishing Data
A CIP record of this publication is available from the British
Library

TO LOVERS

You are entering upon what is probably the most thrilling adventure in life. Certainly, it should be a time of extreme pleasure.

If you want to enjoy to the full your new rôle be careful of the snares and pitfalls. This little book sets them out in a few words. It will help you to recognise them before they occur.

CONTENTS

I

ADVICE TO LOVERS

THERE is nothing half so exhilarating in life as falling in love: but an old adage says that "the path of love is only strewn with roses for those who tread it cautiously." Thus, if you want to enjoy your love-making to the full, there are several "don'ts" that you must carefully observe.

Love-making is, of course, a serious business. No doubt, you will embark on it light-heartedly, as we all do. But don't be too hasty in professing your admiration by words or looks, and don't bind yourself until you are reasonably sure that the two of you were made for each other.

But, when you are sure of yourself, when you know that you have really fallen in love, then don't let your courting be a half-hearted affair. It should be the most thrilling and adventurous time of your life, and if you are wise, you will make it so.

On one thing be determined, maintain a level course in your affections and don't allow them to rise and fall as the barometer does in an English spring. If you blow hot and cold, there is something wrong somewhere and you must ask yourself if yours is really love.

Don't fail to play your part in what is, after all, the only honourable way. Some seek the pleasures of courting as a means of passing a glamorous week-end, whilst others respond to the thrill without taking the trouble to question their emotions and finding out whether they are well-founded or not. Such people are a danger, since they are apt to cool down and cause their rejected partners a deal of fretting.

Having made as certain of yourself as you possibly can, enter upon your courtship with all the exhilaration that you can command. And, let it be an unselfish courtship—one in which you think more of your partner than you do of yourself. Some people will tell you to keep your lover guessing for a good while. But we say that such a course is unworthy. Once you have made up your mind, set full sail ahead and show your lover, by word and deed, that you return his or her affections to the full.

It should hardly be necessary to remind you that courtship is, in effect, a preliminary to marriage, and marriage is for the term of your natural life. Therefore, a step taken in the wrong direction now may alter the whole course of your existence.

Be critical at the outset. The perfect lover is seldom the perfect husband or wife. Perfection rarely comes to lovers except by previous experience. They have courted many times before and, more than likely, they are swayed by the sight of a fresh face. Some time hence, your own face may fail to please when

compared with another. Therefore, don't put too much faith in what might be called "the perfect lover".

Regarding the financial status of your partner, much could be said. Generally speaking, you will be happier with someone in your own station of life than someone who is considerably above or below it. But it was a wise sage who first said that "Love in a cottage is better than riches without love in a palace". In short, whatever you do, don't marry for money.

The remark is often made that "Everybody loves a lover". This is true up to a point. The lovers, however, who become so intoxicated with the new sphere in which they tread so lightly that they neglect the ordinary things of life, are not loved. In fact, they are voted a nuisance.

Therefore, if love upsets your usual routine, throws your work out of gear or makes you neglect your relations and friends, then it is time that you mended your ways. There is only one thing to do and that is to struggle back to a normal existence. You can do it, unless you are one of the hysterical sort.

And, then, there is another thing. Courting is something that should be done in private. To sit with your lover and carry on your love-making openly is an indelicate act. Nobody wants to see you do it and, even if you don't mind, they do, and you are making it awkward for them.

Concerning the ages of engaged couples, a good many opinions have been expressed at various times. Some say that no disparity in years should exist between two people contemplating marriage, whilst others speak of instances by the score where May married December and lived happy ever after.

If any rule can be stated, it is that a man should be older than his wife by anything from two to nine years. But it is a rule we should not hesitate to break if our hearts dictated a different course.

The whole point is that, usually, two people of widely different ages cannot see eye to eye with each other: the younger may want to indulge in active pursuits when the older one feels the need for a quiet existence, and so on. But, of course, if May and December are sure of themselves and are so enraptured with each other that both appear perfect to the eyes of the other, then there is nothing more to be said. Let them join hands and make each other happy.

It may sound contrary to the dictates of charity, but we say this very definitely: Don't become engaged to a person out of pity, even though there is a saying that pity's akin to love. No real good ever came out of a courtship based on pity. It is a partnership that is bound to crash in the end.

And this brings us to a further matter. It is decidedly wrong to become engaged to a person who has some serious affliction of health. It must be recognised that engagements are a preliminary to marriage and marriage ought to entail parenthood. To bring children into the world of tainted stock is not only a crime against society but it is a cruelty to the children. Many people faced with this problem say: "We'll marry, but not have any children." The folly of such a pact becomes more and more manifest as the days roll on. To start married life with the avowed intention of not having children is to ask for bitter disappointments later in life.

The last hint in this general survey is specially directed to our girl readers. It concerns the engagements of British girls with men of foreign nationality. When such a union is contemplated, the greatest care needs to be exercised. In many countries, the laws place women in a very inferior and precarious position. For a girl to submit herself to such conditions, may result in her being stranded at some future time. In any case where such a union is proposed, legal advice should be sought.

II

Do make certain before committing yourself that you are in love with a particular person and not with love itself. Many a man who has been turned down by one girl loses no time in paying his addresses to another, thus showing that he was not as much in love with the one girl as with love itself. Having once enjoyed the thrill and the excitement of the pastime he is determined to have more of it.

Don't delay falling in love until you have reached middle age. Provided financial circumstances permit, and wisdom backs your choice, to get married early is desirable, since young people can more easily accommodate themselves to each other than when they have grown older and their ideas have become fixed.

Don't also delay on the ground that you wish to have a good time first. This implies that in your opinion marriage, instead of being the happiest state, is a sort of kill-joy existence. You'll probably find that if you hold this view the opposite sex will keep clear of you, since, if you expect little, it follows that you have little to give.

Don't marry because the man or girl is, in your opinion, not half a bad sort. The person to marry is not the one you can get on with but the one you can't get on without.

Don't forget that lovers always see each other under the most favourable circumstances. Each is doing his or her level best to please and to appear in a favourable light before the other. There is a good deal of common sense in the old Danish proverb: "You must judge a maiden at the kneading trough and not at the dance."

Don't imagine that the perfect lover, whether male or female, will come along ready made. If they do, mistrust them, since this shows a certain amount of previous experience. The whole time of courtship is a period during which each of the two fashion themselves into each other.

Do be careful before you pass from the friendship stage to that of courtship that you have not been too much influenced by environment and similar circumstances. The girl or man who looks such a dream on the pier may not be at all desirable as a workaday wife or husband. Use your reason to decide whether you will have the same feelings on a foggy wintry day as you have when standing by the sea shore in the glamorous light of a summer moon.

Don't allow yourself to fall into the common error of thinking that if your lover has certain bad habits you can eradicate them after you are married. If he won't alter them when he is in the heyday of love there is little chance of him doing it afterwards, and his love is certainly not strong enough to stand the strain of years. Put him on probation for a fairly lengthy period, and if he fails, then bid him goodbye. Don't be led by your love to giving him a second or third try.

Don't forget to choose your wife in the same way that you would a knife, that is, look to her temper.

Don't accept a man who says that he is going to marry and settle. Make him settle first and marry afterwards.

Do beware of falling in love with a man whom other men dislike or, in the case of a man, with a girl with whom other girls will not be friendly. Generally speaking men and women are pretty fair judges of their own sex and their opinion is one which should be carefully considered.

Don't consider, if you are a man, that you are eligible for marriage unless, in the first place, you are able to support a wife and possible children. Similarly no girl should consider

herself fitted to take up the post of a wife unless she has had adequate training for that profession and can run a home successfully. A pretty face is all very well, but it should be backed up by the knowledge of what to buy and how to prepare it when bought.

Do bear in mind that married life will not be all calm sailing on a summer sea. There are such things as sudden storms and hidden perils, and it should be your endeavour to be prepared as far as possible for all such contingencies. Don't forget that married life has been very aptly described as a great sea for the voyaging on of which no compass has yet been invented.

Don't forget that, in spite of the fact that he is the wage earner, matrimony presses less hardly upon the man than the woman. One aspect of this is shown in the fact that marriage brings with it a greater element of captivity for the woman than it does for the man, and therefore she should be doubly careful before she makes her choice.

Don't be too conceited because you consider that in your sweetheart you have secured the flower of the flock. Make a few inquiries first to see if she is, also, at home among the flour in the kitchen.

Do realise that in youth the natural tendency is to mate; and that, in this, propinquity is a great factor. The girl or boy with whom you are brought into daily contact may seem to be everything that is desirable, but go carefully until you have also seen what is round the corner. It may seem a prosaic way of putting it, but no girl would buy a hat, or no boy a cycle, after looking at only one style or make. They would certainly first make a round of the shops before they came to a final decision.

Don't, if you are a girl, marry a man much younger than yourself. You want a man to protect you, not one that you might mother. Moreover, don't forget that in later years the difference will be more apparent since there will be many recreations in which he can still indulge but which will be closed to you.

III

THE PURSUIT

DON'T, if you are of the male sex, think you are a great and mighty fellow whose manifold charms could not be withstood by the fair lady you have deigned to pursue. She is more expert by nature in the game than you are, and probably marked you down as her prey long before you had any ideas on the matter.

Do take care, my dear young lady, not to let the possible husband rush matters at the outset. To be easily won is to be lightly valued. Take to heart the words of Sir Walter Scott: "The lover's pleasure, like that of the hunter, is in the chase, and the brightest beauty loses half its merit, as the flower its perfume, when the willing hand can reach it too easily. There must be doubt; there must be danger."

Do be careful also to let him do his own hunting. Don't show an eagerness to meet him half way or otherwise he may think that he's such a fine fellow that he could do better elsewhere. Let your tactics at first be those of retreating rather than advancing, but take care to strike the happy medium and not retire too far. Womanly intuition will usually guide you as to the exact spot at which to call a halt.

Don't think that a parade of your many virtues will always attract men. Generally speaking the majority of them are much more susceptible to silk stockings and flattery. Don't forget that the last of these two is nearly always a sure winner. Truly did the poet write:

Man flattering man not often will prevail,
But woman flattering man can never fail.

Don't, if a girl, turn down other possibles until you are quite sure of the one and only.

Man is by nature both covetous and imitative and in consequence will always seek what others find desirable. The more rivals he has, the more he is spurred on to secure the prize.

Don't rush after a particular person of the other sex because so many other men or girls have the same object. To do so, of course, appeals to your sporting instinct, and there is certainly a great delight in getting ahead of others, but it is well to remember that marriage is not a game that can be played over and over again, but one that lasts a lifetime. Moreover it often happens that the much-sought-after person is not, in consequence, entirely free from vanity and selfishness. There is a lot of truth in the old saying that many of the fairest and sweetest flowers blush unseen.

Do remember when you meet a girl with whom you feel you would like to run in double harness to follow the old hunting field advice: "Don't rush your fences." Let your advances be slow but sure. To tell a girl the first time you see her that you are in love with her is not a compliment but an impertinence.

Don't make the mistake of thinking that you must have a lover because all your friends have one. To allow this to be a reason clearly shows that you have not yet sufficient sense to be able to choose a satisfactory partner. Wait and see what fate offers you. Precipitation only too often leads to disaster.

Do take every care to find out something about the other person's disposition before you start to pursue her with the idea of marriage. As far as possible look for a partner with tastes similar to your own but whose disposition is different. In such a case you will become complementary to one another.

Don't look for perfection in your partner. It is a quality that doesn't exist in the world, and if you think you have found it your eyes are probably blinded by love. Moreover, if you do find it, the possessor will also be looking for the ideal of the other sex and you won't come up to that standard.

Don't look for a partner in one who has been brought up with the idea that nothing should stand in the way of the gratification of his or her wishes or caprices. Such a person will hardly find it possible to consult, nor fall in with, the wishes and conveniences of someone else.

Don't let prettiness be the only quality that you seek in a woman, for if it is, your love is more of the senses than of the heart. Bear in mind that many a beautiful soul is to be found behind a somewhat plain face, and that this quality is constant, while beauty, only too often, disappears with the advance of time.

Don't think because you are rather a good-looking young man that you can pick and choose as you please. In the choosing of a future partner, women are normally much wiser than men, and will give greater weight to moral than to physical qualities. You may easily find to your surprise that, although you are a fine tennis player and a great favourite on the courts, you have been beaten by some quiet individual without any claim to good looks.

Do remember the old saying about not being off with the old love before you are on with the new, but be even more careful that you are not on with the new before you are off with the old. In the first case you may be only disappointed because you fall between two stools, but in the second, when the old hears of the new or the new of the old, you are pretty certain of getting a bad time.

IV

DON'T forget that courting time is a period when all should be well with the world so long as you are together. Make it a golden period, without storm or trouble, to which you can always look back with the happiest of memories.

Do be careful to realise that, while a girl may demur at the first kiss, this is probably not because she has an objection. On the contrary, she may be very desirous of it, but she realises that half the pleasure lies in the anticipation, and she's not going to miss a fraction of it. On the other hand if the "no" is decided the only course for the man to pursue is to go and

try elsewhere—in which case it is probable he may be called back and the original decision be reversed.

Don't attempt kissing in a canoe unless you are both able to swim and the lady is prepared to risk the spoiling of her smart summer frock.

Don't let your sweetheart labour under the idea that kisses are singular. She'll appreciate them the more if you make them plural.

Do avoid, whenever you spend an evening together, filling up all the time by talking of yourself, your hopes and your aspirations. If you do too much of this, the girl may come to the conclusion that she has no desire to fill the rest of her life acting as audience to a one-man orchestra.

Do realise that there is nothing so dangerous to the tender passion while still in the bud as a surfeit, and that the time to say "good night" is while each of the two is still desirous of more of the other's company. To go beyond this is to run the risk of love being buried in the grave of boredom.

Don't imagine that quarrels are a necessary part of love. It's all very well to talk about the blissfulness of the subsequent making up, but too frequent disagreements will pall in time. Further, the making up is largely a matter of temperament, and there is always the danger that a rift may become wider and wider.

Don't forget in the matter of kissing the very wise advice given by Herrick in the following lines:

Give me a kisse, and to that kisse a score;
Then to that twenty, adde a hundred more;
A thousand to that hundred; so kisse on,
To make that thousand up a million;
Treble that million, and when that is done,
Let's kisse afresh, as when we first begun.

Although written many, many years ago this advice still stands as good as ever to-day.

Do bear in mind when there's any mistletoe about that two heads are better than one.

Do be careful in your courtship to make

the most of your opportunities. Remember that women are like flowers, a little squeezing makes them the more fragrant.

Don't neglect an opportunity of being charming. Remember that it's the girl with winning ways who comes out best in the game of love.

Don't imagine for a minute that the rest of the world are tremendously interested in the progress of your courting. They've seen the same sort of thing a hundred times before, and it's hardly probable that you will take a line that's original.

Do take care, on both sides, that before entering into any engagement you have made as full inquiries as possible with regard to health, financial status, habits, tastes, etc. Only too many couples enter into a life compact without knowing anything of each other beyond their respective tastes in sport. To know something of a man's tastes is very essential to a girl since she will be more at the mercy of his than he of hers.

Don't go out in a sailing boat with your lover if you've had little or no experience of the sea. Sea-sickness is not attractive, and a green complexion is certainly not one that elicits admiration.

Do take care if your lover proposes to spend a day in the country to go suitably dressed. High heels and frocks that are easily spoiled are not the best kit for rough ground or hill climbing, and to wear the former may mean that you have to give up owing to aching feet before half the proposed journey is accomplished. Let him see that you have an idea of the fitness of things.

Do remember before you make your final choice that it is very inadvisable to marry any-one who laughs at your parents. If this is done in the early stages of your love it is pretty certain that it won't cease with your marriage but rather increase, and such a wounding of your feelings hardly coincides with a deep affection.

Don't be too ready to break a promise you have made to someone because your lover

wishes something else. You may think this will please him, but on the other hand there is a grave danger that he may think you hold your promises lightly. Explain the circumstances to him and keep your pledged word.

Don't meet your lover at six o'clock and spend the time until eight grumbling about the hard work of the office or the way in which your employer told you off. Your lover probably has his own troubles of this kind to bear, and the time that you have to spend together can surely be better employed than in one long grouse.

Don't have a film courtship and build your romance on what you see on the screen. Life isn't so dramatic as it's there portrayed, but usually contains several hundred days of quiet humdrum happiness to each one of drama. Probably you will also find it wiser to save some of your shillings towards the purchase of that future home.

Do be careful that when you have been refused by one girl you don't rush off and, to show that you don't care, at once make love to some other. In doing so you are very liable to be caught on the rebound, and to offer your hand and heart to some one who normally would have had no attraction for you, but whose acceptance of you salves your wounded pride. Don't make the mistake of cutting off your nose to spite your face.

Don't rush into a courtship simply in order to show your independence, or to get even with your parents, or because most of your friends are attached and you are feeling somewhat lonely. Wait until you have thought it out calmly and logically and are perfectly certain that the girl you have in mind will give you all that you desire in a wife. Don't forget the French proverb that it is the first step that costs, since once your name becomes associated with a particular lady it is very difficult to withdraw.

Don't make the mistake of trying to educate your lover in the early, or indeed in the later, days of your courtship. What she wants is a

lover, not a schoolmaster, and if you try to act in the latter capacity you may find that so far from giving a lesson you may receive one, and that in how to take a dismissal gracefully.

Do be careful that you don't follow the advice of those women who think that it's a good thing to keep a man waiting and consequently turn up late for every appointment. To do so implies in the first place that you have little consideration for his feelings, and in the second that you are not so anxious to see him as you pretend to be.

Don't attempt to kiss your lover with your hat still on your head, young man. To do so is to put yourself in the class whose knowledge of what is correct is almost negligible.

Don't boast to your lovers about your successes with the other sex, especially if any of those mentioned are known to you both. In the first place it is caddish to kiss and tell, and in the second the sight of the one-time favoured one will always be a reminder that there was a time when you were not the one and only.

Do be content with your own particular form of recreation and don't insist too urgently that your lover should take it up. To have a recreation in common is very desirable, and no doubt in order to please there will be a certain amount of concession, but don't let there be any suspicion of driving or compulsion. Be content with the fact that your partner is sufficiently unselfish to put personal desires on one side for a time and leave your recreation to make its own appeal.

V

Do bear in mind that while it is quite permissible for a girl to send "speechless messages" with her eyes to the one and only man it is not quite the thing to give the glad eye to all and sundry.

Don't forget that there is a very big difference between courting and flirting. One is attention with intention and the other attention without intention.

Do take every care, if you are a girl, to steer clear of the male flirt. He is nothing but a pirate in Love's waters, and to sail in his company for even a short while on the voyage of life is fraught with danger. Every girl would do well to take to heart the sound advice given by that American humorist, Josh Billings: "Don't hav anything tew du with the boys unless tha' mean bussiness."

Don't fail to give a wide berth to the young lady whose principal occupation in life would appear to be Scouting for Boys. It's also probable that you may find that she belongs to the Ancient Order of Gold Diggers.

Don't ever allow yourself to get the reputation of being frivolous. It's one of the easiest reputations in the world to acquire, and one of the most difficult to lose. Don't forget the words of the old Roman sage written over 2,000 years ago, but equally true to-day: "Levity of behaviour is the bane of all that is good and virtuous."

Do realise, my dear young lady, that unjust though it may appear, it is far more necessary for a woman to be careful of her conduct than it is for a man. In this connection don't forget also that appearances will often injure just as much as real crimes, especially when

people are not inclined to put a charitable construction on them.

Don't forget that the same pack which contains the Ace of Hearts also contains the Knave.

Don't imagine that blue eyes and crinkly hair or, in the case of the other sex, red hair and dimples, are all that is necessary to form a perfect soul mate. Look for such qualities as loyalty and steadfastness that will stand the strain and stress of stormy weather.

Do remember that the seaside in summer is the happy hunting ground of the flirt of both sexes. Take every precaution against sunstroke or, the even more dangerous moonstroke.

Do be on your guard against the sweet, unsophisticated young thing who, when she has known you about ten minutes, confides in you that, with the exception of yourself, she is misunderstood by the whole world. In spite of her apparent childlike innocence she is the most dangerous of all flirts.

Don't forget, my dear young lady, that the

girl who is inclined to flirt outrageously, or to ape masculine manners, is simply and wilfully throwing on one side her greatest asset. In the first case the great charm of womanhood lies in a certain amount of reticence, and anything which lessens this tends to diminish her value in the eyes of the other sex. As regards the second it is a well-known fact that no man desires a bad caricature of himself.

Don't imagine, once you are engaged, that your fiancé will be delighted if you are the recipient of a good deal of admiration from other men. Once a girl is engaged no true gentleman would pay court to her, and to allow those who are not to do so is to lower her own standard and to insult her fiancé. Don't make the silly mistake of allowing other men still to run after you with the idea that this will enhance your value in his eyes.

VI

THE LANGUAGE OF LOVE

Do be careful not to judge the sincerity of your lover only by the fluency with which he tells his love. There is an old, and often true saying, that "one expresses well only the love he does not feel". Most men and women have in them a certain amount of desire to act the dramatic, with the result that affection told in halting and broken sentences is often much deeper than that which trips readily from the tongue.

Don't expect from each other during the period of courtship a high and lofty standard of conversation. Don't insist upon talking all the time about the books you have recently read or the scientific subject in which you are interested. You will probably find that the theme that will interest the lady most is some variation of: "Do you love me and if so how much?" and after all, that is a subject in which you are both most interested.

Don't forget that love's language is always on the side of the extravagant and is hardly framed for the rough wear and tear of everyday life. Many a lover swears that he would willingly die for his loved one, but when it comes to the test his affection sometimes proves to be of the undying order.

Don't bring the language of love too much into use when you are in the presence of others. It is one thing to show affection and another to be sickly sentimental. However much you may love your future partner it's scarcely necessary, when in the company of others, to call him darling in every sentence.

Do take great care not to dub your lover with a pet name that is distinctly inappropriate. There is more than a chance of people smiling if a man calls his hefty, hockey-playing lover his "little popsy-wopsy", or she hails her six-foot big and brawny lover as "Sweetie".

Don't make the mistake of assuming that because you have told your lover that she is too pretty for words you won't get the words if you annoy her, or if your devotion is not all that it should be.

Do remember that to lovers love itself is usually such a solemn thing that it doesn't permit of the introduction of humour. Lovers take themselves very seriously, and let but one party laugh at some protestation or remark of the other—however absurd it may be—and Cupid is very likely soon to take flight.

Don't, in a spirit of false humility, be constantly telling your lover that you are not good enough for her. It's probably quite true, and in the years to come you may prove it over and over again, but it's not wise or polite to run yourself down at the very start.

Don't make your letters nothing but notes of admiration. Although you are in love you should not cease to take an interest in the world around you. Every girl likes an occasional repetition of the fact that to one person she is all the world, but too much is likely to produce a feeling of satiety. The sensible modern girl likes to be treated in a sensible manner.

Do endeavour, also, when writing to your loved one to steer clear of poetry since she will hardly be interested in the feelings of some one she did not know. What she will love to hear is that you are all impatience till you can see her again. More especially don't attempt verses of your own. They will read very differently if brought up against you in ten years' time by your wife. Moreover, if anything happens to upset the engagement, in the case where the writer has put in his own poetry the jury will usually give a verdict against him without leaving the box.

Don't, on the other hand, run to the opposite extreme and confine your communications to each other to post cards and telegrams. A girl will much prefer to hear that life is very dull without her to receiving a picture post card announcing that the house shown thereon is the hotel at which the writer is staying. If two people are really in love with each other any description of the daily doings of one will be full of interest to the other.

Do remember that really nice girls should never discuss make-up secrets with their lovers. If he compliments you on your nice complexion let it go at that, and don't giggle and say that you bought it at the chemist's. It is not candour, but the height of foolishness, when a girl attempts to step down from the pedestal on which her lover has placed her.

Don't forget there is a big difference between the language of friendship and the language of love, and there should be no using of the second of these two until the parties are engaged or have come to a mutual understanding.

Don't talk about any physical ailment or other trouble from which you may suffer. The mention of such is nearly always a blow to love. No man who looks upon a particular woman as an angel likes to hear his angel announce that she's sure it's going to rain because her corns are hurting so badly.

Do take care that your conversation doesn't display a jealousy of other girls. This is small-minded and petty, and, if you have won the man of your choice, you should have no reason nor space for such feeling. Besides, what you say may have the effect of interesting your lover in the person of whom you are jealous and then anything might happen.

Don't treat your loved one to too much baby language. He probably won't mind a little of it, but its use on all and every occasion will soon make him restive. After all he has a certain dignity to maintain as the future head of a household and to be constantly asked: "Did ums want to do this?" or "Did ums want to do that?" is not conducive to doing so.

VII

Do be careful not to rush into a proposal, or, if a girl, into an acceptance, as the result of a momentary impulse or the influence of surroundings. Things often look different in the cold morning light to what they did in the glow of the twilight. Take care that there is careful consideration by both parties. Many a man has tied a knot with his tongue that his teeth will not loosen.

Don't be afraid to get married. Surely you are as brave as your mother, and she wasn't afraid. It may be that it entails a good many sacrifices on your part, but that should be more than compensated for by the joys of

57

companionship it brings with it. If you are certain that your choice is right, pluck up your courage and propose.

Don't spend a lot of time puzzling how, and in what manner, you shall propose. You are not out to make a theatrical display but to get the job done. If you are certain you have made a right choice the words will come alright. Popping the question is very much like a bottle of champagne, if it doesn't pop of its own accord it isn't much use.

Don't make the mistake of being too long before you put your fate to the test. There is often the danger of the other fellow getting in first. Once you have decided that she is the one and only girl for you, drive ahead to secure her. She will know your feelings quite as well as you know them yourself, so don't be like a cork and leave her the task of drawing you out.

Don't preface your proposal with some long statement as to your own unworthiness. If you are such poor stuff as you would make yourself out to be you have no right to ask the girl to marry you, and if you are not what object is achieved by decrying yourself? Go straight to the point and ask the girl to marry you. She has probably decided long before whether or not you are up to the required standard, and if she hasn't shown any disinclination to your presence it's probable you have passed the test satisfactorily.

Do refrain most carefully from making some long statement as to your hopes, desires, ambitions, etc., before you come to the actual question. You are there to make a proposal, not to deliver an oration. Moreover don't forget that the girl is waiting anxiously to know whether you mean business or not.

Don't make semi-proposals which leave the girl in the awkward position of not knowing where she stands. Don't ask her meaningly if she can cook when you know that you are not in a position to supply the things to be cooked. If your income doesn't justify marriage in the near future, but you are afraid of losing her if

you don't speak, tell her frankly the situation and ask her boldly if her feelings for you are sufficiently strong for her to wait for you.

Do avoid the modern craze for eccentricity, and its companion, notoriety. Don't try to make your proposal in some strange and unusual place. It may be original and thrilling to do it in some weird manner, such as while flying, but it won't be half so satisfactory as when performed sitting side by side on the good old-fashioned sofa.

Don't follow the old-fashioned practice of going on your knees to a girl when you propose. No man looks at his best in that position, and the modern girl would probably laugh at you. Instead of going on your knees you will find it much more satisfactory, and much more likely to be successful, if she is sitting on yours.

Don't forget that it's much easier to make a proposal than it is to withdraw from one. It's not a game at which you can play fast and loose. As one cynical writer puts it: "Man proposes but woman makes him stick to it."

Don't endeavour to be ultra-modern and casual in making your proposal. Don't imagine that any nice-minded girl is going to say "yes" to such a proposition as: "Well, what about a spot of double harness, old thing?" To every girl a proposal is a serious matter, as on her acceptance or refusal of it hangs her future happiness, and to treat it in a light matter is an insult to her.

Do take care, my dear young lady, not to be one of those girls who say "no" at first, knowing all the time that they mean ultimately to say "yes". This is sometimes done under the idea that by accepting at once they would seem to give themselves too cheaply, but it is liable to the danger that the man may go off and not return, unless you have taken the precaution to lock the door.

Do endeavour, if the answer to a proposal is to be "no", to give it in as gentle a manner as possible. To youth the thought that all his endeavours to charm have been in vain, the realisation that he does not come up to what

the lady desires, or, even worse, to the standard of some other man, is a crushing blow. Try to make it as gentle as you can.

Don't treat any proposal—if given seriously —with levity. It may be that it is quite impossible, and even absurd, but it must be remembered that in asking a woman to be his wife a man pays her the greatest compliment that he can, and it must be treated as such.

Don't follow the one-time absurd practice of saying: "This is so sudden," or "It's the last thing in the world that I expected." Generally speaking, you have known that the man has been in love with you even before he knew it himself so why pretend otherwise?

Don't, if refused, try to get the lady to change her mind by vowing that life for you is ended and remarks of that nature. They are more likely to raise feelings of contempt rather than those of pity. Take the verdict like a man and a gentleman. After all it won't probably be long before you have a second try or you meet some other girl who can heal the breakage.

Don't, further, if refused with disdain, accuse the lady of having led you on, encouraged you, etc. A better way, and one which will give you your revenge, is to apologise and say you only did it for a bet.

Do remember, however, that if there is no one else who is ahead of you in the running, and provided the refusal has shown no great dislike to your person, it is quite probable that you may succeed in a second attack. Remember the words of Byron:

But yet she listened—'tis enough—
Who listens once will listen twice,
Her heart, be sure, is not of ice,
And one refusal no rebuff.

VIII

Do be careful when you become engaged not to look round on the rest of the world in a superior manner as if no one had ever been in the same condition before. This is a disease which you will get over in time, but in the meantime you will be a source of amusement to those around you.

Don't forget that familiarities in public are in extremely bad taste and that the fact that you are engaged does not excuse them.

Don't introduce or speak of your fiancée as "my young lady". This gives the impression that you are anxious to assure your listeners that she really is a lady, a point which they are quite prepared to take for granted.

Don't buy the ring without some previous consultation with the lady as regards her wishes. Remember it is going to be her most prized possession and therefore let it take the form that she most desires.

Do be careful not to ask your fiancée to your home to meet your family until they have called or written and asked her to visit them. Once you have announced your engagement to them it is then their duty, unless they object to the engagement, to give her a welcome, in one of these two ways, to the family circle, and until they have done this she cannot very well thrust herself upon them uninvited.

Don't let the engagement ring be of the showy variety. At the present time good taste favours a narrow circlet of gold or platinum with one good stone surrounded by very small brilliants.

Don't forget that if for any reason the engagement is likely to be a long one it is not usual to make any public announcement, the information only being given to the more intimate friends.

Don't, if newly engaged, sit with your hands in your lap or fiddle with your ring in such a way as to draw people's attention to it. It is, of course, a great and wonderful possession to you but you can't expect others to be equally interested. Try to realise that such a possession is not unique; a few million girls have worn them prior to you.

Do endeavour when among other people not to monopolise each other. Of course, no one's company or conversation is equal to that of the loved one, but at the same time there are others whose claims on your notice cannot in common courtesy be disregarded. Do remember that such monopoly is a form of extreme selfishness and shows a lack of consideration for others.

Don't be constantly using endearing epithets to one another. A too lavish use of them only tends to make a couple ridiculous. Try to keep both your conduct and your language dignified.

Do be careful, Miss Newly Engaged, that in your pride of possession you do not make the mistake of keeping your lover ever at your side and only allow him to go away when you send him on some errand. As a rule he will be only too glad to be around, and to fetch and carry for you, but it is better that this should be on his own initiative and not at your word of command. Let him realise that though you belong to each other you are still free agents.

Don't attempt to shower expensive presents on the lady of your choice directly you become engaged unless the wedding is to take place in the near future. In such a case they can be included among those given by bridegroom to bride. Until that happy day arrives they should be confined to such less expensive articles as flowers, sweets and similar gifts.

Do take care not to make your one topic of conversation the perfections of your loved one. He or she may be all that you paint, but if you do you must not be surprised if your eulogies are met with a smile or, in some cases, with a yawn.

Don't, when you become engaged, put on a superior attitude towards those of your girl friends who are not. To do this is in the worst of taste, and approximates to boasting of the power of your own charms. Moreover, in the case of any of them who have been unfortunate in their love affairs, it is often downright cruelty.

Don't be suspicious, but, on the other hand, don't take everything on trust. Even the best of us are, under certain conditions, prone to attempt to paint black white. If before an engagement each party to it investigated as closely as a careful prospective employer does before engaging a new secretary there would be far less unhappy marriages.

Do start as you mean to go on. Don't commence on such angelic lines that you cannot possibly keep it up. Some men who will fetch and carry all day for their fiancée during the first few weeks of the engagement

71

will leave her to open the door for herself six months later. Take care that the houri of the engagement period doesn't become entirely the housekeeper of the married one.

Don't hesitate to break off an engagement if you consider you have made a mistake. To go on with it out of consideration for the feelings of others is both foolish and wrong, since it will mean that two lives will be spoiled. Where a cancellation of the engagement does take place the man should always in courtesy take the blame for the rupture, and neither party should, under any circumstances, discuss the cause of the cancellation. Where the engagement has been announced in the Press a notice as follows should be inserted. "The marriage arranged between Mr. John Smith and Miss Blanche Williams will not now take place." Needless to say with the ending of the engagement all presents should be returned.

Don't think, even if you are engaged, that it is quite correct for you both to go for your holidays to the same hotel or boarding house.

This is certainly often done, but it is far from being the correct thing. The only occasion when it is really permissible for an engaged couple to stay together in the same house is when they go to a married friend of one of the parties. In other circumstances they should stay at different houses.

Don't let the whole period of your engagement be one round of gaiety and amusement, and don't let your only endeavour be to have a good time. Remember that this is largely a time of probation, during which you should do your best by studying each other's ways to prepare yourselves for the years that you are to spend together. Don't waste it in frivolous amusements and go to the altar practically ignorant of how your future partner acts in everyday life.

Do bear ever in mind that from the commencement of the engagement the honour of the girl is in the man's hands. This is a sacred trust, and if his love is really pure he will never allow her to do anything on which people might comment. He must never forget that her reputation must be to him far dearer than his own.

Don't forget that where the somewhat modern practice of introducing the prospective bridegroom to his fiancée's friends by means of an At Home is adopted, the invitations should be sent out by the girl's mother. At the same time the girl is at liberty to invite her own friends by means of a personal note. When this At Home takes place the girl should stand near the door of the reception-room to greet her friends, to introduce where necessary to her mother, and then to introduce her fiancé.

IX

Don't encroach upon your privileges as a lover. Don't, in the happiness of long evenings with your loved one, forget that poor old Dad is sitting up, sometimes in the kitchen, until you see fit to take your departure. Remember that he may be a man who likes to go to bed early.

Don't labour under the idea that her father will be tremendously surprised when you announce that you wish to marry his daughter. In view of the frequency of your calls, and the usual length of your stay, he would be even more surprised if you didn't.

Don't seek your wife among your own relatives if you can possibly help it. Go further

afield. Marriage, where there is a blood relationship, is very risky, and the complication of relationships is never desirable.

Do remember that, even if a girl is living apart from her family, it is only courteous for her fiancé to write to her parents directly the engagement takes place and express the hope that it meets with their approval. An early opportunity should also be taken of satisfying them of his ability to maintain his future wife in a similar position to that to which she has been accustomed.

Don't make the mistake of starting your married life by living with relatives. Even if you can't get, or can't afford, a house, take two rooms in preference, or otherwise wait until you can. It sounds very easy to become one of the family, but it rarely ever works successfully. The period immediately following marriage is one in which the two of you have to learn to fit into each other, and this is not easy, but it's three times as difficult if one of you has, in addition, to learn to fit in with a new family.

Do endeavour, also, not to have business dealings with your new relatives. To do this may, at first, seem very satisfactory for both parties, but in the case of a disagreement neither party is so free to act as they would be in the case of one outside the family, and only too often the business relationship will ultimately injure the family relationship.

Don't rely on the financial help towards your marriage that you will get from the rich uncle. These good people have rather a habit of not doing what is expected of them and turning out indeed near relations.

Don't either of you start off with the idea that your mother-in-law is going to prove a constant source of trouble. Even the comic papers have now dropped this idea as being behind the times. If you do your parts fairly towards each other the mothers on both sides will be only too content in the thought that you are happily married.

Do beware of the girl or man who run down their own people. To do so is to show an

absence of family loyalty, and if this quality does not exist there is a great probability that loyalty to husband or wife will not be a predominant feature. Don't conceal things that the other party ought to know, but even in that case content yourself with a plain statement without any observation of your own.

Don't, my dear young lady, expect the whole household to be subordinated to your fiancé. Don't always tell your sister that she can't have her friends in on a particular night because you expect that he will be coming. Let him realise that there are occasions when the rest of the family must be considered.

Do try on both sides in visiting the house of the other's parents to accommodate yourself as far as you possibly can to their habits and ways. Great as his or her love may be it is subjected to a heavy strain when you make it apparent that you think the old people are fifty years behind the times. To use a very modern expression: "Watch your step." Make a few inquiries beforehand. If father is a Die

Hard Tory don't tell him you are an extreme Socialist. If mother has strong religious views don't make a point of announcing that you see no difference between one form of worship and another.

Don't ignore the small brother. He can be either a strong ally or a very powerful enemy. It is not meant by this that you should bribe him, for if you are weak enough to do this he will probably levy a regular toll upon you, but treat him more as a pal. The fact that one older than himself does this will flatter him and cause him to eat out of your hand.

Do be careful to be courteous to all your future relations. Don't snub Aunt Jane because you think she's such an old frump. It is well to remember that in thirty years' time the coming generation will think just the same of you.

X

DON'T expect, no matter what trouble you take, to be able to keep your engagement secret. Eyes, actions, etc., are giving you away all the time to intelligent and interested observers and troth, like truth, will out.

Don't imagine that because the loveliest girl in the world has said "yes" to you that you can rush round at once and tell all and sundry what a lucky fellow you are. You must remember that age-old custom has given to the lady the privilege of announcing the engagement and you must not take from her that right.

Do remember that although in these days the young lady no longer refers her lover to papa, but consents or refuses irrespective of what he may desire, it is still an act of courtesy for the parents on both sides to be told at once. This will normally be done by a personal visit to the girl's home at which the young man will ask for their consent and at the same time give some particulars as regards his financial position. As previously explained, in the case where the girl is living some distance from her family this should be done by letter. In any case no public announcement should be made until the parents on both sides have been apprised.

Do take the utmost care that all relatives and close friends are notified quickly, and always before mere acquaintances. Many near friends feel very aggrieved if they do not receive notification until perhaps a week after the news has become common property.

Don't forget that where a dinner is given to celebrate the engagement the invitations should *not* state for what purpose it is held. The announcement should be made during the dinner, but no speeches are necessary since the matter is more of an informal and family affair.

Don't attempt to strike an original note in any announcement in the Press, as custom has laid down the correct form to be used. Further, don't make a Press announcement unless your position is sufficiently good to warrant it. The announcement should take the following form. "A marriage has been arranged (and will shortly take place) between Mr. A.B., son of Mr. and Mrs. C.B., of Portrush Cottage, Luton, and Irene, daughter of Mr. and Mrs. E.F., of Grantham Hall, Sandgate." The words "(and will shortly take place)" are only added when the date of the wedding has already been fixed.

Don't be upset if some of the congratulations you receive are not as whole-hearted as you would have liked. Jealousy still exists in the world, and it may be that you have acquired a prize that others were desirous of gaining.

Don't simper or giggle when congratulated by friends, and above all don't rush into a eulogy of your future partner. Such a proceeding may result in a quiet smile—after you have left—especially if the person to whom you have been talking knows your lover or loved one well. Besides, don't forget that as he or she now belongs to you, you are committing the social crime of praising your own. Rest content with a quiet and dignified letter of thanks.

Do take care that all congratulatory letters are answered at once. To wait until you see the writer, and then thank personally, is not good form. It is up to you to take as much trouble in replying as they did in writing.

Do also remember that when it is your turn to write letters of congratulation on an engagement, that to the girl should not congratulate her, but rather express the pleasure that the news has given you, not forgetting your best wishes for her future happiness. On the other hand, one to the man should always convey the note of congratulation, the assumption being that he receives benefits while the lady gives.

Don't commit the unpardonable error, when giving your girl friends the news, of telling them what he said and what you said on this important occasion. This is thoroughly bad form, as all that was said then should be held sacred. Further, if you are so unwise, your friends will probably quietly laugh at you, but your fiancé won't if his words ever come back to him.

Don't expect your news to be received with surprise and as if it were some information of national importance. Probably your friends who have, in the meanwhile, been looking on, have been expecting it for some time, while on the other hand the announcement of the engagement of two people, though of supreme importance to the parties concerned, does not usually stagger humanity.

Do remember that, as a general rule, it is not advisable for a girl to convey personally the news of her engagement to some man whom she has previously rejected. The news will naturally not be pleasing to him, and to

convey his congratulations will be somewhat of a difficult ordeal. Further, it will be almost impossible for her to keep the note of happiness out of her voice and this will give additional pain. Leave the news, if possible, to come to him from a third party, or, if this is not possible, convey it in a brief letter.

XI

GETTING THE HOME TOGETHER

Do realise from the outset that it puts a great strain on love if you have saddled yourself with so many responsibilities under the hire purchase system that your monthly salary will be mortgaged for several years to come.

Don't forget that, as a first step, it's much better to rent a house in a district with which you are yet unacquainted than to buy one. It may happen that with increased knowledge you find the area for many reasons unsuitable.

Don't rent or buy a house simply because it looks nice. Have it examined by a competent authority.

Do, unless you have plenty of money, insist on a quiet wedding and so save expense. A swagger wedding isn't a pleasant memory, if, directly after the honeymoon, you have to commence thinking of economy in means and ways.

Do be careful not to overload yourself with furniture at the commencement of keeping house. Furniture has a habit of accumulating, and, if you sell, the price you get will be very different to that which you paid.

Don't, unless you are asking for trouble or unhappiness, take a high-class house, or buy high-class furniture, on a low-class salary.

Don't commit yourselves to rushing into a lot of entertaining until you see, by trial, how your expenses are going to work out.

Do arrange beforehand with your wife that all bills shall be settled weekly. Small bills, even for newspapers, have a habit of growing quickly.

Don't omit in estimating your expenses to allow a good margin for doctor's bills and unexpected calls.

Don't forget to arrange your expenditure in such a way that your wife will have two separate allowances, one for the housekeeping and one for dress and personal expenses. Arrange this definitely before your marriage.

Do take care to instruct your future wife—if she requires the knowledge—in such subjects as house assessments, electricity, rates, etc. If possible she should pay gas, electricity and coal bills, and by so doing she will realise what an important factor they are and the need for economy.

Don't lose your friends by delaying, or not acknowledging wedding presents.

Do be careful, if you are not keeping a servant, to discourage your friends from giving you presents of silver articles. Silver cleaning is a bugbear; it takes up precious time which might be spent out of doors and spoils pretty hands. Moreover when the little toddler gets the measles the cleaning of it has to be suspended and dirty silver is always depressing.